Raffi Songs to Read™

SHAKE MY SILLIES OUT

Illustrated by David Allender

You Are Entering
MARIPOSA FOREST
BEWARE of SILLY ANIMALS

Crown Publishers, Inc., New York

For Justin and Joel

Published by Crown Publishers, Inc., 225 Park Avenue South, New York, New York 10003, and represented in Canada by the Canadian MANDA Group
CROWN is a trademark of Crown Publishers, Inc.
RAFFI SONGS TO READ and SONGS TO READ are trademarks of Troubadour Learning, a division of Troubadour Records Ltd.
Manufactured in Italy

Library of Congress Cataloging-in-Publication Data
Raffi. Shake my sillies out. Song; unacc. melody. Summary: A song in which the singer declares, "Gotta shake my sillies out, clap my crazies out, and wiggle my waggles away."
1. Children's songs. [1. Songs] I. Simpson, Bert. II. Simpson, Bonnie. III. Title.
M1998.R   87-750478
ISBN 0-517-56646-X

10 9 8 7 6 5 4 3 2 1

First Edition

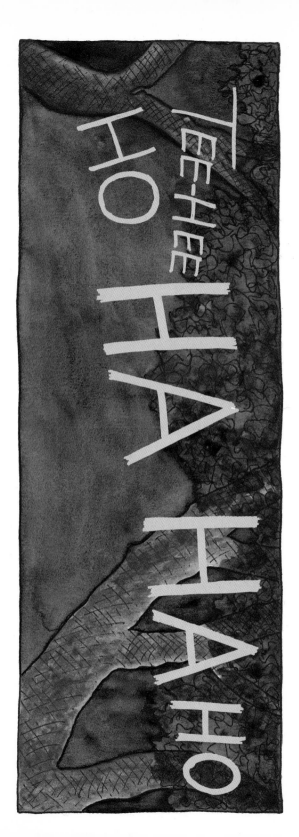

Gotta...

shake, shake, shake my sillies out,

Shake, shake, shake my sillies out,

Shake, shake, shake, shake my sillies out,

And wiggle my waggles away.

Remember, Blue Jays, there are fierce animals in the forest, such as bears and....

Gotta clap, clap, clap my crazies out,

Clap, clap, clap my crazies out,

Clap, clap, clap my crazies out,
And wiggle my waggles away.

Gotta jump, jump, jump my jiggles out,

Jump, jump, jump my jiggles out,

Jump, jump, jump my jiggles out,
And wiggle my waggles away.

Gotta yawn, yawn, yawn, yawn my sleepies out,
Yawn, yawn, yawn my sleepies out,
Yawn, yawn, yawn my sleepies out,

Yawn, yawn, yawn my sleepies out,

And wiggle my waggles away.

Gotta shake,

shake,

shake my sillies out,

Shake, shake, shake my sillies out,

Shake, shake, shake my sillies out,

And wiggle my waggles

away.

SHAKE MY SILLIES OUT

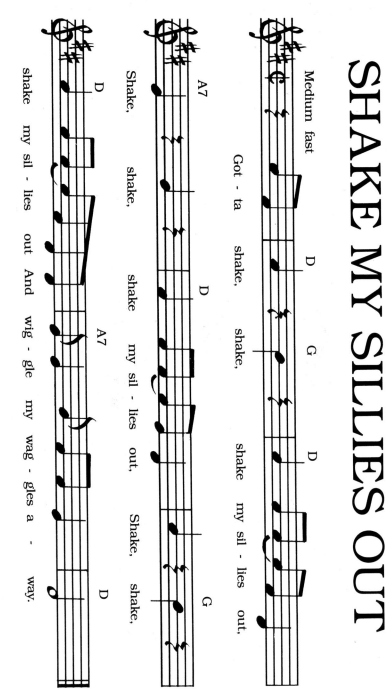

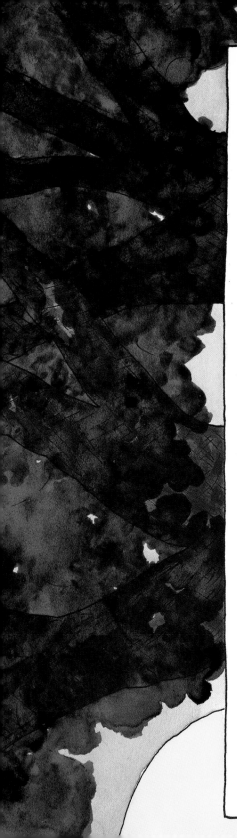

2. Gotta clap, clap, clap my crazies out,
Clap, clap, clap my crazies out,
Clap, clap, clap my crazies out,
And wiggle my waggles away.

3. Gotta jump, jump, jump, jump my jiggles out...

4. (Slower) Gotta yawn, yawn, yawn my sleepies out...

5. Gotta shake, shake, shake my sillies out...

Music by Raffi   Words by Bert and Bonnie Simpson